Everyday 3-D Shapes

Spheres

by Laura Hamilton Waxman

illustrated by Kathryn Mitter

Content Consultant: Paula J. Maida, PhD,
Department of Mathematics, Western Connecticut State University

magic
wagon

visit us at
www.abdopublishing.com

Published by Magic Wagon, a division of the ABDO Group, PO Box 398166, Minneapolis, MN 55439. Copyright © 2013 by Abdo Consulting Group, Inc. International copyrights reserved in all countries. All rights reserved. No part of this book may be reproduced in any form without written permission from the publisher.

Looking Glass Library™ is a trademark and logo of Magic Wagon. Printed in the United States of America, North Mankato, Minnesota.
042012
092012

Text by Laura Hamilton Waxman
Illustrations by Kathryn Mitter
Edited by Rebecca Felix
Series design by Craig Hinton

Library of Congress Cataloging-in-Publication Data
Waxman, Laura Hamilton.
Spheres / by Laura Hamilton Waxman ; illustrated by Kathryn Mitter.
pages cm -- (Everyday 3-D Shapes)
Content Consultant: Dr. Paula Maida.
ISBN 978-1-61641-877-9
1. Sphere--Juvenile literature. 2. Shapes--Juvenile literature. 3. Geometry, Solid--Juvenile literature. I. Mitter, Kathy, illustrator. II. Title.
QA491.W3785 2012
516'.156--dc23
                           2012007120

This shape rolls on floors and ground.

Big or small, all spheres are round.

Look around for this shape's look.

Search for spheres inside this book.

5

Find tasty fruit with a nice round shape.

Juicy orange and purple grape.

7

Do you see the shiny beads?

Spheres can be as small as seeds!

Spin this sphere round and round.

See which country can be found.

Spot the small spheres made of glass.

Marbles roll in the short grass.

Blow sphere bubbles light as air.

Look! One landed in Jill's hair!

This sphere is heavy. Will Ben win?

He needs to knock down one last pin.

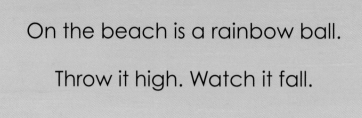

On the beach is a rainbow ball.

Throw it high. Watch it fall.

19

Sticky spheres taste sugary sweet.

Lick them up for a yummy treat.

Spheres aren't just inside this book.

They're all around you. Take a look!

I Spy a Sphere Game

Look around. Find a sphere. Then say, "I spy a sphere that is . . ." and name its color. Everyone has to guess what sphere you see. Then it is someone else's turn to spy a sphere. You can guess what it is.

Count the Spheres Game

Choose a room in your home. Count how many spheres you can find.

Glossary

marble: a sphere made of a hard material and used in games.

rainbow: something that has many different colors.

round: something that is circular in shape and has an equal distance from the center to any part of the edge.

shape: the form or look something has.

sphere: a shape that is round like a ball.